Aisha's Moonlit Walk

Aisha's Moonlit Walk

Stories and Celebrations for the Pagan Year

Anika Stafford

SKINNER HOUSE BOOKS
BOSTON

ISBN 978-1-55896-485-3

Printed in the United States.

Cover design by Kathryn Sky-Peck.

17 16 15
6 5 4 3

Library of Congress Cataloging-in-Publication Data

Stafford, Anika.
    Aisha's moonlit walk : stories and celebrations for the pagan year /
Anika Stafford.
        p. cm.
    Summary: Best friends Aisha and Heather and their families celebrate var-
ious pagan holidays together. Includes discussion guides and activities.
Includes bibliographical references.
    ISBN 1-55896-485-1 (alk. paper)
    [1. Holidays—Fiction. 2. Neopaganism—Fiction. 3. Best friends—
Fiction. 4. Friendship—Fiction.] I. Title.

PZ7.S779Ai 2005
[E]—dc22
                                                2004026681

Let my ritual be in the heart that rejoices, for behold—
all acts of love and pleasure are my rituals.
—Starhawk, *The Spiral Dance*

Contents

Dear Reader,

You might be surprised to know that many contemporary families turn to pagan rituals to celebrate the seasonal holidays and to teach their children the foundational values of paganism, an earth-based religion whose major themes are common to most religious faiths, both ancient and modern. These values honor our connections to the earth and each other, our commitment to social justice and activism as a spiritual practice, and our belief that all parts of the self are sacred--body, mind, emotions, and spirit--and that the centrality of the Goddess/God is manifested in all of life and its cycles.

Given the nearly universal appeal of these themes, the stories and activities in this collection are for anyone who wishes to celebrate the passing of the seasons in an earth-based spiritual way. You may be a pagan parent who would like stories for your children that reflect your spiritual holidays. You may be a teacher who would like to honor spiritual diversity and help counter negative stereotypes of paganism in your classroom. Perhaps you are not associated with any group but simply seek stories and celebrations about our shared journey through the year.

Aisha, a young girl, celebrates the pagan holidays with her family and friends. In these stories, the terms witch and Wiccan are used to describe people of a sect of the pagan faith. Many pagans of today hope to rehabilitate these terms: A witch is a good thing, these stories teach us, and so is a Wiccan. They reflect a pagan experience that children can relate to and understand. If you plan to use the activities, be sure to read "Guide for Parents and Educators" at the end of this book to learn about leading a circle. If you teach in a secular environment such as a public school, you may wish to omit the spiritual rituals. You can also adapt the activities and rituals to suit the needs of your group or practice. The "To Find Out More" section at the back of this book offers materials for readers who want to learn more about the wide range of traditions and interpretations that are included in paganism.

I wish each of you joy and blessings on your spiritual path. Whatever it may be, I hope this book helps to bring you nourishing community, wondrous solitude, and a good dose of pleasure.

Blessed be,

Thank You, Milly!

Samhain

Tonight is Halloween. My family and I walk up to the hill by our house. We're headed toward the park, where we'll meet all of our friends for the Samhain ritual.

I can smell leaves burning in a bonfire. It's a little chilly and the moon is bright and full.

It's Samhain, the Witch's New Year, the time when the Old Year is dying and a new year is being born. It's a special time of the year when pagan people can feel close to their beloved dead. My family has been part of the Wiccan religion since before I was born.

I didn't want to come this year. I didn't even want to leave my house. My mom told me, "Aisha, I know you're sad, but it will be okay to be sad there. Just come with us, even if you don't really feel like it right now."

So I'm walking to the park with everyone. I wipe tears from my eyes and pull my jacket tighter. Everyone is in costume.

1

My mom is dressed like a giant bird. She loves to dress up in silly clothes.

My dad does too. He wears the same jester hat every year. It even has matching shoes. My brother is dressed like an elf. He's been singing all day. Loudly.

I don't want to sing. I don't even want to get candy. All I want is Milly. She was the best dog in the world—and I want her back with us.

Until two weeks ago, Milly would run to the door to greet me every day when I'd get home from school. She would flop onto her back and roll around for me to pet her tummy. She would know whenever I was sad or scared, even if she was in the other end of our house. She would hurry to come lean on me, and then she would just sit there and smile until I felt all safe and warm. She was almost fourteen years old, but I still thought of her as a puppy.

When she died we buried her under a tree in our backyard. We call it Milly's Tree now. I've cried every day since. I've been sleeping with her collar and her favorite toy. I'm bringing them to the ritual tonight. My dad walks over and puts his arm around me while we walk. I realize that I've been holding Milly's things so tightly my hands are in fists. I loosen them enough to put an arm around my dad. We walk up to the park on this chilly, crisp night.

The park is filled with people dressed in brightly colored clothes. There are lanterns in all different shapes and sizes. Most of the people are here for a big Halloween party, but there are so many pagans here that we have our own celebration over by the pond.

My best friend, Heather, and her moms are the first to see us. They run over, yelling, "Happy Samhain!" and give us big hugs. My brother runs around everyone, singing, "It's

Halloween, it's Halloween, run and dance and yell and sing." He sings until Heather picks him up and gives him an airplane ride. They both laugh.

Heather walks dizzily over to me after the airplane ride. She tucks her arm through mine. "Look," she whispers, really excited. Heather is excited a lot. "They set up the maze from last year again!" Last year there was a really fun maze made out of tree branches, and big hanging sheets. "I can't wait to walk through it!" she squeals, clapping her hands. There is something kind of magical about everything here tonight. Maybe it's okay that I left my room, even though I didn't want to.

There is a bonfire in the clearing by the pond. There are people playing drums and flutes and calling everyone together to form a big circle around the fire. People dance and sway their way over to where the ritual will begin.

A woman dressed all in green stands at the North corner of the circle. "Spirits of the North, spirits of earth," she calls out, "that which makes our bodies grow strong and our food rise from the ground. Be here now." People come forward to put their special things on the altar facing North. My mom puts sunflowers on the altar in memory of her dad, who loved to garden. I think of Milly's Tree in our backyard. I want to put Milly's things down too, but I can't stop holding them tight.

At each point in the circle someone calls to one of the four directions. "Spirits of the East, of air, strong storms and gentle breezes, come clear our minds." There is only a gentle breeze in the air tonight, but I feel like there's a strong storm in my belly. A woman facing South speaks in a loud, excited voice: "Spirits of the South, of fire. Creative flickering flames, come be with us tonight and set our spirits free!" I remember burying Milly. My mom and dad said, "It's okay for your spirit to go now," to her.

A man dressed all in blue stands facing West. His voice is deep and clear: "Spirits of the West, of water, of running streams, still lakes, and the powerful ocean. Be with us tonight as we cry, as we laugh, as we grieve and celebrate." Heather's mom Tara walks forward and places a necklace made of beautiful blue stones on the altar facing West. It is in memory of her grandmother, who used to live on an island.

"Come to us, come to us, come to us," we all sing. I remember playing with Milly in a cold, running river last summer. I feel the music run through me. I am still cold, and I'm starting to get goose bumps.

People all around the circle begin to call out the names of the ones they would like to honor tonight. "Blessings to Cerridwin, faithful cat." "Blessings to Kate, to your sparkling spirit." "Blessings to Anne, may you finally be free from pain." Milly's name catches in my throat and I am crying again. I feel a little silly with so many people around.

Now people are calling out wishes for the New Year. "May we have strong roots like the trees." "May we protect our precious water." "May our love bring healing to this world." I think about how much love I felt sitting with Milly's head on my lap. All I can think to wish for is to have that feeling back, but I don't see how that can happen.

Slowly, everyone finishes calling out their wishes. The circle opens at one end and we start to move, winding ourselves into a giant spiral. We sing and look each other in the eyes as we pass.

"We all come from the Goddess and to her we shall return, like drops of rain flowing to the ocean." I notice tears in other people's eyes and now I don't feel quite so silly.

"Hoof and horn, hoof and horn, all that dies shall be reborn." I change the words of this part to "paw and horn." A few people notice and smile. "Vine and grain, vine and grain, all that's cut shall rise again." During this part I walk very low and then jump up every time we sing the word "rise."

When we are all wound up in our spiral, people drop hands and dance. I move and dance too. The song melts into a hum. I look up at the big moon and at everyone's hands reaching up to it. Our humming showers down in a hundred different notes. I edge my way to the altar at the center of the circle and place Milly's toy and collar on it. I smile.

Eventually everyone thanks the four directions, opening the circle we'd cast. We hold hands and yell, "Merry meet, merry part, and merry meet again!" We put our hands on the ground and feel how close we are to the earth. Everyone moves away from the circle. They go to share food, play games, and celebrate being together. Even though I know there will be candy for all of the kids, I stay behind. I go sit down in front of the center altar and stare at Milly's things.

I sit by myself. "Thank you," I say to Milly. "Thank you for having been our dog. Thank you for being so much fun to play with and for always knowing when I was sad. Thank you for trying to follow me onto the bus that day, even though you weren't sup-posed to." As I thank Milly, I begin to feel safe and warm instead of cold and sad. I begin to feel tons and tons of love, right down to my belly. "It's okay to go," I whisper. I let go a huge sigh and lean back on the cool grass.

After a few moments Heather comes running over. "Aisha," she says, panting, "I just went through the maze! It's so cool, and they give you candy at the end." She holds out her hand to help me up. "Come walk through it with me, I want to go again and again!" I take her hand, and together we walk through the maze. Then we climb a tree and eat our candy way up in its branches.

The warm love in my belly heats me up. It makes me all excited and silly, like Heather. We scoot down to lower branches on the tree and hang upside down by our knees, laughing our heads off. We stay and play for a long time.

Late in the night we walk home. My brother rides on my dad's back, too tired to sing anymore. I have Milly's things tucked safely into my jacket pocket. I take my mom's hand and we walk home in silence, all of us full of magic, love, wishes, and candy.

Things to Talk About

◼ In the story, people call out their blessings to their "beloved dead." What blessings do you wish for your "beloved dead"? Let everyone have a chance to say her or his blessings out loud.

◼ At the end of the story, Aisha thanks Milly for all the ways she was a special part of her life. Do you have a person or pet in your life that is special to you the way Milly was special to Aisha? What things could you thank him or her for?

◼ How did Aisha change from the beginning of the story to the end? Have you ever changed like that? What happened in your life?

◼ The people at the ritual call out their wishes for the next year. What would you like to ask for in the next year? You can begin this talk as a lead-in to the witches' brew activity below.

Celebrations

Please see the "Guide for Parents and Educators" at the end of this book for ideas about setting up a general altar and creating and closing "sacred space." The following suggestions are for creating a Samhain space on your altar and celebrating this holiday.

Make witches' brew. Get a cauldron and fill it with several different kinds of fruit juice (it works well to have one natural, sparkling fruit juice for fizzyness). At this time of year you can find little Halloween cauldrons at just about every grocery store. The cauldron traditionally was thought to be a place where life, death, and dreams were brewed together by the Goddess. Give each person a small cup of juice. Hold your cups and imagine something you'd like to "brew" in your life over the next year. Any request is fine as long as it is not a request for something to happen to another person (for example, asking for more close friendships is okay, but you should not ask that a particular friend develop more feelings for you). As you each pour juice into the caldron, say what you are hoping to bring into your lives. Imagine your requests being brewed together as you mix the juice into a Samhain fruit punch. Pour some for each person and drink together!

- **Honor your beloved dead.** Find pictures and symbols of beloved people in *your* lives that have died (yes, pets definitely count). A symbol could be a baseball glove of a person who loved to play, or a favorite toy of a pet. If you do not know anyone who has died, you can tell stories about your ancestors. Get together, light candles, and tell your stories as you place each item on your altar.

- **Carve pumpkins.** In old pagan traditions, carved pumpkins were meant to be lights helping our "beloved dead" find their way home. After telling stories of your beloved dead, talk about what kind of pumpkin carvings would be welcoming to those spirits. You may wish to carve one pumpkin to place in the center of the altar, or carve separate ones.

- **Sing.** Z. Budapest wrote the song "We All Come from the Goddess." It is sung on the CD *Chants: Ritual Music from Reclaiming and Friends*, which is available at many pagan/new age/alternative bookstores (see page 80). "We All Come from the Goddess" can be fun to sing together as you imagine the drops of your juice pouring into the cauldron being like drops of rain pouring into the ocean.

The Longest Night

My parents have invited all our friends to a giant sleepover because it's Solstice night, the longest, darkest night of the year. Usually Heather and I have our own sleepovers, but tonight it's different. When Heather's family arrived, both her moms said, "Happy Solstice, Aisha," and gave me big hugs. But Heather and I aren't speaking.

Last week we had a big fight. When we found out we were trying out for the same part in the school play, we ended up yelling at each other in front of everybody. We've been ignoring each other since.

On this longest darkest night of the year, the wind whips and hollers outside our windows as everyone comes bumbling in, all bundled up. Our friend Alex, the storyteller, and all five of his housemates rush to huddle to-gether on our couches and get all toasty warm.

Alex's little girl, Jessica, is three years old, like my brother Eli. The two of them run around the house with mistletoe. They jump up to hold it over people's heads and shriek and laugh. But not Heather and me. Our parents talk and laugh, but Heather and I don't even sit together.

Our friend Rupie appears. Her hair is wild and crazy around her face from riding her bicycle in the wind. She worms her way onto the couch, wrapping herself in blankets. Rupie lives by herself in a little apartment with three cats. Heather and I both want to be like her when we are old enough to have an apartment. But tonight, I only talk to Rupie when Heather is talking to other people.

By early evening, our little living room is full of big-voiced people nestled close. Evergreen boughs hang all over our walls, filling the place with cedar and fir spice. We've set up a winter altar in the middle of the room, and our sleeping bags are circled around it. The altar is an old box that we all painted together on Winter Solstice last year. On the altar are ocean stones to honor the water, and feathers and incense to honor the sky. We have potted herbs for the earth and a bright red candle-holder filled with red candles to honor fire. Everyone is snuggly and warm, except Heather and me.

On this longest darkest night we sleep with our heads facing the altar. We all nestle into our sleeping bags and into the circle. Everyone eats warm, yummy food.

Before sleep we gather around the altar in a circle. Alex puts a large sheet of paper down on the floor and starts to talk. "With everything so cold and dark outside," he begins, "Winter Solstice is a time to turn inside and dream about what we want to plant when the light returns. It is a time to leave some things behind." He pauses. "Let's share some things we want to leave behind in the dark."

Rupie goes first. "I want to stop being so busy that I can't spend any time with my friends," she says, looking directly at both Heather and me and then writing it on the sheet of paper. Heather and I avoid looking at each other. What if we aren't best friends anymore?

"I want to stop being so serious all the time and write more fun stories," Alex says as he writes. Alex is the best storyteller in the whole world.

We go around the circle, and everyone says one thing they'd like to say good-bye to. I don't say anything when it's my turn. I am thinking about our fight. I want to write that I hope Heather stops being a play hog, but we can only wish things for ourselves, not for other people. Instead of talking, I just light a candle on the altar. Heather does the same thing.

Alex takes out another sheet of paper. "After today, the light will start returning," he says. "What do we want to welcome into our lives as the light returns?"

"We want lots of cookies!" Eli and Jessica say at the same time, laughing. And again, everyone goes around the circle. And again Heather and I stay quiet and light candles. We put the papers up on our living room walls and we stand arm in arm around the altar. Together we take a big, deep breath and blow out the candles.

On this longest darkest night the adults stay up late and talk. Some of them stay up all night to greet the sun. Tonight I go to sleep early. It's no fun to stay up all night when Heather and I aren't whispering and giggling. Falling asleep, I feel like the cold night is inside me even though the living room is warm and filled with friends.

In the middle of the night I wake up suddenly, gasping for breath. My stomach drops like it did when I fell off the swings at school. In my dream Heather and I were trying to climb a mountain, but we kept pushing each other off until we fell. I look around the room. There's no mountain, just our living room. Our friends are sleeping and snoring. Eli and Jessica have their heads across Rupie's ankles, just like her cats. Alex sits in our enormous round wicker basket chair, wrapped in a blanket, writing as usual.

But I can't go back to sleep. What if I have that dream again? I grab my journal and go into my room to be alone. I want to yell and stomp. I want to wake up Heather and start fighting all over again. But she hasn't done anything wrong, really, it was just a dream. I pace around my room, sputtering under my breath. I push open my window and call out to the wind, "This is the worst Winter Solstice ever!" The wind whistles around the big pine trees in our yard.

I crumple against my bed. I write, "Heather and I had such a big fight, maybe we won't be best friends anymore." I slam my journal shut. The cover is decorated with bright stars and moons that Heather and I painted on it last Winter Solstice. Looking up, I see a pressed-leaf mobile hanging in my window. Heather and I made it together last Fall Equinox. My room is cluttered with poems and pictures, sculptures and statues that we made together. And we never fought about those. Not once.

Outside, the night is dark and cold. I sit on my bed, staring at the closed journal. I think about Heather asleep in the other room. I think about how long we've been friends.

If Heather and I can write together instead of fighting about who's the best writer, then maybe, I think, just maybe . . . . If we can paint stars and moons together instead of fighting about who has the most art supplies, maybe we can work this out. Just maybe. I tiptoe back into the living room. I find the first sheet of paper, now taped to the wall. "I want to say good-bye to fighting with Heather about plays, not to being best friends," I write. My letters are big and bold. I put the pen down and stand back to look at my words. There, in the corner, I see that Heather has written, "I want to say good-bye to fighting with Aisha." This makes me so happy! I want to run over, hug her, and make up right then. Instead, I tiptoe over to the other paper. I write in more big, bold letters, "I want to write plays with Heather instead of fighting about them."

I hug my journal close to my chest and take a deep breath. Over in the wicker chair Alex is still awake, and I squeeze next to him. I have known Alex my whole life.

"I'm just finishing a story about being best friends," Alex whispers. "Maybe tomorrow I can read it to you and Heather." I smile and nod, knowing somehow Heather and I are still best friends. Alex puts down his notebook and looks out the window. I look out too. We can still see the moon on one side of the sky, but the sun is peeking up too. This longest night is almost over.

Suddenly I am sleepy. Even though it's almost morning, I lean against Alex's thick, woolly sweater and pull the blanket up over me. Winter Solstice night is ending. I feel cozy and warm inside. Watching the frost shining bright in the sunrise, I fall asleep.

Things to Talk About

▓ This story is about the darkest and coldest time of the year. What things do you do during the winter? Are there special things you can do now that you can't do during any other season?

▓ In this story, Aisha has had a big fight with her best friend, Heather. Have you ever had a big fight with someone in your life you care a lot about? Some people think fighting feels like a "dark" or "cold" time, just like winter. How do you feel when you've had a fight?

▓ How did the fight change for Aisha at the end of the story? Are there special things that can happen from fighting, even when it feels "cold?"

▓ During the story, people think about what they will do when the light returns. They talk about "listening" deep inside to know what they want. Even when it's dark outside, there is a "light" inside us that we can listen to. That light is in you too. You are a part of the Goddess/God. How do you make winter a "warmer" time for the people in your life? How has someone else made winter a "warmer" time for you?

Celebrations

▓ **Find some green.** This is the time of year when much of nature is resting; much of what is usually green now lies dormant. Take some time to walk around your neighborhood and see what green you can find. Is there holly where you live? Evergreen trees? See if you can find some boughs and clippings to take home and decorate your altar.

▪ **Find some journals.** When we turn inward, we need a place to record our thoughts and feelings. Find inexpensive journals for everyone in your group. Those who may not be able to write yet can still use a journal for drawing and painting. Spend some time decorating your journals together and talking about what things you can use it for. You may wish to discuss the idea of recording your dreams and why people often find this useful. Place the decorated journals on your altar.

▪ **Make divine mirrors.** Get one small mirror and one frame for each person. Collect pictures and objects from nature. Make sure to have plenty of art supplies as well. Each person will place a mirror inside a frame and decorate it. In advance, print up little pieces of paper that say "Goddess," "sacred," "divine," or any other words that may mean this idea. You may want to write your names on pieces of paper as well. You may also add these words to their mirrors in recognition of the divine within themselves that brings "light" to the world during the winter. While making the mirrors, discuss what it can mean to be part of the divine. Talk about how, in pagan tradition, everything in nature has beauty and is sacred or holy. Each of us is part of nature, as beautiful and sacred as the earth that grows our food or the trees that give us air. You may also wish to play pagan chants and sing together while you make the mirrors.

New Kittens

I arrive at Heather's house early on Brigid's Day to help her and her moms set up for tonight's celebration. It will be at their house.

February 2nd is Brigid's Day. Brigid is a creativity goddess. The sun is getting stronger every day now, and Brigid's Day is our festival of lights. Heather and her parents and I have lined up candles all around the house. Tonight we'll light every one until the rooms flicker in the dark. Some people will paint, some will sing, lots of people will dance. They'll glow in candlelight as they make something special.

We have barely begun setting up when our grown-up friend Rupie arrives in a rush, her hair flying from her bike ride through the freezing wind.

Coming through the door, Rupie practically shouts, "I'm wondering if there is someone here named Heather and someone here named Aisha who would like to come see the pregnant stray cat I just rescued?" Immediately we drop what we're doing and put on our jackets, not even thinking that we could miss tonight's celebration.

It's a long way to Rupie's, so we take our bikes. I haven't ridden since I fell off and cut my lip last summer. I hate the sight of blood, so I've been walking instead of riding. But I want to see the new cat so badly, I don't care.

Rupie's kitchen smells like oatmeal and chocolate, but there's no cat. We walk into the living room. It's piled high with books and papers, but still no cat. Rupie starts calling, "Here kitty, kitty, kitty." We look under the bathroom sink and in the hallway closet. There is no cat anywhere.

Finally Rupie stands by her bedroom door quietly. She motions us to come look. We can hear the sound of purring. "Shh," she tells us, and we tiptoe into her room. We look where Rupie is looking. Behind a potted plant in the corner, on a pile of old blankets, is Rupie's new cat. Her belly ripples as she pants and purrs, squinting her eyes.

"She's having her babies!" Rupie whispers. We all stand there staring. Finally Rupie says, "Do you want to watch?"

Heather and I squeeze hands. We always squeeze each other's hands when something is exciting. "Yes," we squeal as quietly as we can manage. I *am* excited, but something in my belly feels nervous-jittery and I don't know why.

We both phone home to see if we can stay even if it will make us late for the ritual.

"It's Brigid's Day," my mom says. "Do something that will make you strong."

"It's Brigid's Day," my dad says. "Do something that will make you wise."

"Birth is the most creative act of all," Heather's moms tell her. "It's a perfect Brigid's Day ritual."

"What can we do?" Heather and I bounce up and down. But why do I feel scared?

Rupie puts her hands on our heads so we'll stand still. We stand there watching and waiting. Soon it's dark outside. "I have the vet's number in case there are problems," Rupie says, "but she knows what she's doing. Mama cats always do." Rupie squeezes hands with us. The cat is purring loudly, and her belly ripples faster and faster. Suddenly, the top of the first kitten's head starts to peek out. The rest of its tiny body comes out all covered in slime and blood. I want to run out of there. I was so excited that I forgot there would be blood. When I fell off my bike last summer, there was blood all over my shirt and even in my fingernails. I felt sick to my stomach for days.

"This is too gross," I say, turning to leave.

"How could something so small be alive?" Heather whispers. Rupie shrugs. "Magic, I guess." The mama cat starts to lick the kitten's face. We watch as the new kitten takes its first breaths, its eyes closed tight. "It's so, so magic," Heather whispers, just about squeezing my hand right off.

I look away from the blood, but I stay in the room, still holding Heather's hand. The kitten finds its mother's nipple and starts to nurse.

"I'll be okay," I say out loud, "I'll be okay."

But then more slimy stuff and blood comes out. "No, no, no," is all I can think to say as I run out of the room. I know that cats usually have many kittens. There's no way I can look at all that blood.

I think of everyone over at Heather's house now, lighting candles and saying what they're proud of and what they need help with. I wish I were there. "Rupie," I call, "can I light a candle?"

"That would be perfect," Rupie tells me. I find a match and light the candles hanging on her wall. Then I light the candle that sits between figures of two friends holding hands. I turn off all the other lights, and the room begins to glow magically. "May I be able to watch the kittens being born," I ask the Goddess. It is for Brigid's Day.

"She's such a good, strong cat, isn't she?" I hear Heather saying excitedly. "Isn't she a good, strong cat?" I can almost hear her bouncing up and down. I just sit on the couch, not bouncing at all.

But Heather bounds in, grabs my hands, and tries to pull me up from the couch. "I can't believe we're really seeing the kittens being born!" she says. "Can you come back? You can hide behind me whenever you want!"

Rupie comes in and sits next to me on the couch. She puts her arm around me. "This is amazing," she says, "I remember when my cat Oberon was a tiny kitten, still with his mom. I was there when his eyes just began to open. I held my finger over him and he started reaching up to grab it. It was the first thing he saw."

"That is so cool," Heather and I say together.

I look at the candles burning in Rupie's living room.

Heather is still standing there. "Please come back, Aisha," she begs.

I decide to go back, even if I have to look away the whole time.

Watching from Rupie's doorway, we see that the mama cat has just pushed out the third kitten. Looking at the kitten's tiny face, I don't think about the slime and blood nearly as much. Even though I still look away sometimes and hide behind Heather sometimes.

When we jumped on our bikes this afternoon and followed Rupie, our hair flying, I had no idea I would be able to watch so much blood and not feel as sick to my stomach anymore.

"Rupie," I ask suddenly, "do you think maybe I can have one of the kittens when it's older?"

"You have to ask your parents first," Rupie says. I know I said I never wanted another pet again after my dog Milly died, but now I think maybe a kitten would be okay.

The rest of the kittens come out pretty quickly—only about ten minutes between each of them. I watch the whole time, squeezing hands with Heather and Rupie and feeling flickering happiness in me. Heather's and Rupie's smiles are so big, they must feel it too. There are five kittens in all. When they are all washed and nursing, we go sit in the living room. Rupie heats us up some of her winter squash soup and we sit and eat in the candlelight.

Heather's mom Sonja comes over on her bicycle to pick us up. She peeks into the room to see the new kittens. "That is the most amazing creative gift in the world," she says. Heather usually rolls her eyes and shakes her head at me when her mom says things like that, but now she puts her arm around her and looks at the kittens. "Why?" she asks her mom. Sonja pauses. "My favorite kind of creativity is the kind that helps things grow." We look at the kittens. We are full of Brigid's Day happiness.

We put on our jackets and give Rupie good-bye hugs. Sonja asks, "Aisha, did you actually watch the kittens being born? I know you hate the sight of blood."

I shrug and look at the back at lights shining in the living room. "Magic, I guess."

Things to Talk About

- Aisha is scared of blood but wants so badly to see the kittens being born that she finds a way to get past her fears. Is there anything you are scared of?

- Aisha is able to overcome her fears by doing some of the things she has done at previous Brigid's Day celebrations with her friends and family. Have you ever overcome any fears? How did you do this?

- At the end of the story, Heather's mom Sonja says that birth is her favorite creative act because she loves creativity that makes things grow. Everything in the universe grows; you can see creativity everywhere if you look for it. What kinds of creative things do you see around you when you go for a walk? At school? At home? In stores?

- Your birth and your creativity are part of the Goddess/God; they are part of what makes the world amazing. What are your favorite creative acts? What do you love to do? How do you feel when you do these things? Is this feeling a kind of magic?

Celebrations

▦ **Honor the sun's return.** Find or make things that symbolize the sun's rebirth. These things may vary depending on where you live (for example, you might be able to find tulips poking up through the snow on the ground). If you can't find symbolic things outside, making your own works just as well. Wonderful bright suns can be made with crepe paper, colored plastic, and other textured art supplies. What is the sun making reappear where you live? What objects represent this to you?

▦ **Honor your beginnings.** Find pictures and symbols of beginnings in your lives. These could be pictures of your births, the births of pets, baby pictures, or pictures/objects that mark the beginnings of new things in your lives. For example, you may wish to bring your first pair of dance shoes if you are a dancer who has been dancing for a long time, or your first karate belt if you have achieved other levels since. This can be a great time to tell stories about your births, your backgrounds, and where you've come in your lives. Share these stories while you decorate your altar.

▦ **Make poetry cards.** Go through your favorite poetry anthologies and find poems about love and magic. Copy enough poems so that everyone can pick one or two. Of course, you can write your own poem as well, or copy out lyrics of your favorite song about love and magic. Get some nice paper and art supplies and make cards to put the poems in. Read the poems out loud or sing your favorite songs to each other or sing your favorite songs to each other as part of this activity; this way many different kinds of creative gifts can be shared. You can place the cards on the altar when they are done, or trade with each other.

A fun addition to this activity can be to make up your own stories as a group. For older groups, pass a piece of paper around the circle and ask each person to write one sentence on it. The next person can write a sentence and then hide the previous one. This way the person writing sees only the last person's sentence as he or she is writing. Depending on the size of the group, you can go around one to three times before opening the page and reading the poem you've written together. With younger groups, you can go around in a circle and have each person say one line or one word. In mixed-age groups, older children can help write what younger children say. You can make these group poems into poetry cards as well.

Our Rainy Day Play

Spring Equinox is here. It's time to plant. Time to know what you want and make it really happen. Heather and I know already. We want to be actors, and today we're going to put on our very own play that we wrote especially for Spring Equinox. We're going to perform it in Heather's backyard, and we've been planning and rehearsing it forever. Our friend Alex has agreed to be our narrator. Not only have we invited our pagan friends, but we've even invited friends from school who don't understand what it means to be Wiccan or why we celebrate Equinox.

But Spring Equinox morning I wake up to rain! I want to cry. Heather's moms helped us build a little platform stage in their backyard all last week. It was so sunny then that we never even thought about rain.

"What are we going to do now?" I ask my mom.

"Well, Aisha," she says, "maybe you can clear a space in Heather's living room and do the play inside." But I don't want to do it inside after we've built the stage and everything.

"What are we going to do?" I ask my dad.

"You can invite everyone another day when it's sunny and do it then," he suggests.

"But we've invited them and practiced and got it ready for today, for the Spring Equinox!" I tell him.

We've got seeds sprouting in tiny newspaper pots on nearly every windowsill. When they are ready, we'll plant them outside, where the spring rains will help them grow. This is the season for rain! Why didn't we think it could rain on the day of our play?

Heather phones. She says her moms suggested the exact same things my mom and dad did. It's so freaky when our parents do that! She didn't like their ideas any more than I did.

"But I have another idea," she says, "and it's perfect for Equinox. We have a great play, right?"

"Yeah," I say.

"But it's raining," she says.

"I know," I say, groaning.

"Well," says Heather, "isn't that perfect for Equinox? Good things and bad things are in balance! You know what we should do?"

"What?" I ask. "Tell everyone to bring umbrellas and do it anyway?"

"That's exactly what I was going to say!" Heather shrieks. "You've got to be creative for Equinox, otherwise how would anything work? Do you think our friends are crazy enough to watch a play in the rain?"

We call everyone and ask them to bring umbrellas. To our surprise, they all show up! They stand in their raincoats, waiting with their umbrellas, yelling "Happy spring!" and "It's so good to see you." Even our three school friends come. "You've got to be creative for Equinox!" we tell them. They giggle, wriggling close under their umbrellas in the wet.

Heather and I squish around the yard getting ready. "What are we going to do about our costumes?" I ask. "Our props will get drenched!"

Heather runs over to me with plastic bags. "How about these?" she asks. We stuff our costumes in the plastic bags behind the stage. Everyone is watching and waiting.

"What if we slip and fall?" Heather asks, all dripping and bedraggled just as we're about to go on stage. I grab her hands and squeeze them tight. "Let's imagine roots going from our feet into the ground, making us all sturdy, even in the rain." We take deep breaths until we feel steady and ready to go. Then we walk to the middle of the stage and look out at our audience.

"Thank you for coming," I announce. I clear my throat and continue. "It's the Spring Equinox. The day and night are equal right now."

"Winter is over, spring is really here!" Heather continues.

"This play is about getting ready for spring!" we both say at once.

Holding their umbrellas under their chins, our audience claps and cheers. There are only fourteen of them, but they make a lot of noise. Alex begins: "Once there was a young girl who lived in a small town. The town was like many other towns except that it hadn't been spring there for as long as anyone could remember."

We speak our lines in loud clear voices. We wear our dresses with boots and jackets.

Even though we are wet, we perform our play.

Heather and I take turns playing all sorts of characters, pulling on different hats and holding the soggy props.

At one point, when Heather is sitting on the stage, she accidentally kicks up some mud, and it splats on the ground near the audience. We try not to laugh. It's a wet play. A soggy play. But we really make it happen—we really do.

As the play ends, we all take hands as Alex recites, "The people were finally able to welcome in the spring, and as they did, it began to rain. A lovely, loud, luxurious spring rain wet their faces in the night. They were so happy, everyone sang!"

We are getting the giggles again, and this time we can't hold our laughter in. I hadn't even remembered that the play ended that way! We stop being our characters and go back to being crazy old Heather and Aisha, completely drenched and dripping in the lovely, loud, luxurious spring rain. Soon the whole audience is laughing right along with us.

We all raise our hands in the air and begin to sing and dance in a circle. We laugh as mud splashes up from our boots. No one cares about the mess.

This morning I didn't see how the Equinox play could work in the rain, but now I just dance in my big old gum boots, squish-squashing through the wet, wonderful earth. Everyone gives us hugs afterward and agrees that the play is a huge success. Even our school friends say that they think celebrating Equinox is a lot of fun. Then everyone goes inside to eat snacks and get draped in dry blankets. Heather and I will go too, but first we collect some rainwater in two little jars to keep on our altars in memory of our rainy Spring Equinox play.

Things to Talk About

- Aisha and Heather have been working to get their play ready to perform outside, but on the morning of the play it's raining. Have you ever worked hard for something and run into an obstacle you thought would "ruin" everything? What happened?

- Aisha and Heather end up seeing their obstacle as part of good things and hard things being in balance for Equinox. Is there anything in your life that is hard and exciting? How does this feel for you?

- Aisha and Heather decide to use their creativity and sense of humor to find the solution. Have you ever solved a problem this way? What did you do? What happened?

- At the beginning of the story, Aisha says that it's time to plant. It is time to know what you want and work to make it happen. She wants to be an actor. Is there something in your life that you know you want? What can you do to "plant" this goal? You can use this as a lead-in to the planting activity.

Celebrations

- **Collect water.** Set some dishes out to collect rainwater for your altar and for use in your circle. Talk about how the water comes from the sky. Even the water in our taps comes from reservoirs that get filled by the rain. This can lead to conversations about how it is important not to use too much water and about ways you can conserve water. Talk about how all the water we use ends up in our local rivers, lakes, and oceans. When it goes down our drains, when we flush the toilet, all of this water will drain into other bodies of water that are filled with fish, plants, and other aquatic life forms. This can lead to conversations about how we can keep from polluting our water. We are all intrinsically connected to the water, and we depend on it for our lives. Without the water, nothing can grow. You could also visit a stream, river, or lake to collect water. If you are doing your circle as part of a class, you can ask everyone to bring some water from near where they live and then talk about where it came from. Have a pitcher ready on the altar to mix all of your water together.

Make newspaper pots. You only need newspaper, string, and a small, empty glass bottle. Lay the bottle on its side and wrap about four inches of the newspaper around it. Take the bottom of the newspaper and fold it up to reach the top (you may need to trim it depending on the length of the paper). Stand the bottle up, tie string tightly around the newspaper, and take the bottle out. During the ritual, you will place dirt in the space where the bottle was, making a nice little biodegradable planting pot. Discuss how everything we eat depends on good, healthy dirt. The animals some of us eat need to eat grains, which are grown in soil.

Plant seeds. Place a bag of dirt and a scoop next to the altar. Collect some easy-to-grow, organic seeds (bean seeds are particularly good for this). Let each person pick a seed. Holding your seeds, close your eyes and imagine your goal, the thing you know you would like to make happen. Make sure each request is something done by you for you, not a request to change the actions of another person (see the activities for Samhain). Imagine yourself having achieved your goal. What are you doing? Whom are you with? What do you hear? Smell? Taste? Feel? What does this goal look like when you've achieved it? When you have finished, open your eyes. Fill each of your newspaper pots with soil. You are welcome, but not obligated, to say what you are planting as you put your seeds into the water. Pour all of the water into a pitcher and have each person water the seed of the person to the left (you will want to have something under the newspaper pots before you water the plants, of course). As each person pours the water, say, "May all your dreams grow."

The Sea Creatures

Beltaine

It's May 1st! May Day, the day we celebrate Beltaine with all of our Wiccan friends. My mom and dad, my brother Eli, Heather and her moms, and I all pile into the car to go out to our friend Alex's house on the beach for the Beltaine party. Everyone is happy, laughing, and silly as we crowd into our seats.

The grown-ups are all lovey-dovey. They have been smiling, hugging, kissing, and staring at each other with moon eyes all day. Heather and I give each other disgusted looks. "Why are you guys all being so gross?" Heather demands.

"We're not being gross," my dad says. I knew he would say that. "Beltaine is a time to celebrate love. We see that love when we look at each other, and it makes us smile."

Heather's mom Tara turns around in her seat. "We're also happy about it being the

33

middle of spring, when everything's growing. You're growing, plants are growing. I think that's beautiful, and that makes me happy."

I shake my head at Heather. My mom pulls the car out of the garage and starts driving to the beach. Heather shrugs back at me. Our parents are just like that. "Aisha," she whispers, "I still think they're being gross, but I can't wait till we get to play on the beach."

As we pull up to Alex's house, I can see the big maypole in the yard with colorful ribbons around it. There are lots of our friends dressed in bright yellows, reds, greens, and blues. The grown-ups are all as silly and happy as my parents, kissing and giggling and yelling, "Happy, happy Beltaine!" We jump out of the car and are greeted by tons and tons of hugs. Our friend Alex gives the best hugs. He is really tall and always picks us up and spins us around when he hugs us. Heather and my brother and I clamor to get the first hug from him, then we run to the beach as fast as we can.

We race across the warm, soft sand. It squishes between our toes. I can't think of anything better than having friends with their very own private beach, especially on Beltaine! I fall down and let myself roll until I bump into Heather's feet. She trips, but then falls down next to me on purpose. We look at each other and laugh. "Aisha," she yells, even though I'm right next to her, "let's be crabs!"

We walk on our hands and feet, our bodies high in the air until we are close enough to the water that it laps onto our fingers and toes. I shriek and stand up. So does Heather. We run to the ocean again and again. Then I run into the water a little deeper and splash her. "How could you?" she gasps, but she's not really upset. She runs in deeper too and splashes me back.

There's lots of seaweed all around us. I pick some up and squeeze it in my hands. I put some on my head. I drape some on my shoulders. The sun beats down on my back, and the wind from the water blows cold across my wet clothes.

"I'm a sea creature," I tell Heather. I growl and gnash my teeth. I pick up more sea-weed and hand it to her. She drapes it across her head and shoulders and arms too. We growl and run around, kicking the water with our feet.

My brother sees us and runs into the water, yelling, "Me too! Me too!" Heather grabs me by the shoulders and says, "Let's be a three-headed sea monster!" We pick up my brother between us and run out of the water, across the beach, onto our Alex's grassy yard, where we tumble into a pile, laughing and out of breath.

Others have already gathered. They are getting ready to start the ritual. My nose is full of sea smells, and my skin feels all tight from the wind and sun.

I pick up a small drum. Heather chooses a rainstick, and my brother gets a pair of cymbals. We're ready for the circle! We play our instruments and stand facing North. All the kids call out, "By the earth that is her body!" Then we continue around the cir-cle, each facing East, and call out, "By the air that is her breath!"

Facing South, we chant, "By the fire of her fiery spirit." We walk, drumming our drums, clanging our cymbals, and dancing to face West. "By the water of her womb!" We join hands with the grown-ups and form one big circle. Everyone says together, "A circle is cast!" We all cheer.

One by one, we step forward and take ribbons. Alex takes a red ribbon and says, "I take red to bring creative fire to all of my stories."

My mom's friend Alice takes a blue ribbon. "I take blue for healing my body." Alice was in the hospital a few months ago. "Get a green one," Heather whispers to me. We both take green ones.

"We pick green for sea monsters," Heather announces.

"Why sea monsters?" someone calls out.

I look at Heather and I look at myself, still draped in seaweed. "Because they're fun!" I answer. People laugh, a couple cheer.

"For fun!" someone yells back, and more grown-ups kiss.

I look around the circle at big, round women draped in colorful clothes and tall, skinny people in jeans and T-shirts—everyone so different. I look back at Heather with the seaweed on her head. Heather is the weirdest person I know. She is my best friend in the world.

When everyone has a maypole ribbon, a woman walks around the circle, drumming. A slow, steady beat starts. "Why do we dance?" the drumming woman calls out.

"Because everyone is so beautiful" Tara calls back.

"Because our bodies are amazing!" my mom adds.

"We dance to celebrate that all things are connected," someone yells. Heather and I hop up and down, waiting to be able to start dancing.

Half the people in the circle take a few steps closer to the maypole. We begin to dance, winding our ribbons over and under the others. At first the dance is slow. We begin to sing.

"She changes everything she touches, and everything she touches changes." Flowers in the garden are starting to grow. I can smell wafts of roses and marigolds as we dance.

"We are changers, everything we touch can change." The words of the song change a little. I begin to change the pace of my dancing. We all move quickly, weaving our ribbons faster and faster.

The words change a third time. "Touch us, change us, touch us, change us." I let my shoulders bump lightly into the people I pass in our dance.

Our song gets loudest when our ribbons are all wound up. We let them drop and get tied together at the bottom of the pole. We join hands. We link arms. We dance until all we can do is collapse into a circle, sprawled on the grass. Then we are quiet. We are so quiet we can hear bugs buzzing by in the air and the ocean's slow lapping onto the shore. Quiet and still.

A woman starts walking around the circle with a big jug of water. We take turns splashing the water on our hands and faces and letting it soak into the ground.

After a few minutes, the other kids and I pick up our instruments and walk the four directions of the circle in reverse—we start with West and end with North. We thank each direction for being part of our celebration. Then everyone holds hands and yells, "Merry meet, merry part, and merry meet again!"

After we've opened the circle, we begin our feast. We share bowls of fruit, big heart-shaped cookies, and raspberry juice until it stains our lips and tongues all red.

Later, as we get ready to leave, my dad asks Heather and me, "Do you see what I meant about Beltaine now, or do you still think we're being gross?" I think for a moment, then answer, "I don't know if I'll ever stop thinking you and mom are gross when you make moon eyes at each other and kiss, but I do think Beltaine is the coolest holiday ever, and I think it's my new favorite."

Everyone laughs. I've said that after each celebration we've had this year. Still laughing, we walk across the grass, and, creeping like sea monsters, Heather and I climb into the car.

Things to Talk About

- Aisha's parents and Heather's parents show their love for each other by hugging and kissing. Aisha and Heather love each other too, but they show it by how they pretend and play together. How do you show love to the people in your life that you care about? Do you show love in different ways for different people?

- In the story, different people have different ways of feeling good in their bodies. How do you feel good in your body? (For example, you might feel good by dancing, eating, or by playing in the sand or the grass.) When have you felt the best in your body? What things make you feel good?

- In the ritual, everyone sings a song about how the Goddess (or nature) changes everything she touches. What do you see changing around you? In nature? In your families? At school? Could the Goddess be touching these things? The song also talks about being able to change everything we touch. What have you changed with work you've done? Does this mean you are part of the Goddess?

◼ Before they start dancing, everyone takes a different-colored ribbon and calls out why he or she picked that color. Are there colors that make you feel a certain way? Do you remember certain colors when you remember events?

Celebrations

◼ **Use your five senses.** This altar-decorating activity can be done in two ways. (1) Go for a nature walk and try to find something that affects each of your five senses. Find something that smells good to you, something that feels good to your skin, something you like to look at, something that tastes good to you or reminds you of a good taste, and something that makes a pleasing sound. Say what you like about each thing as you put it on the altar. (2) Find personal belongings that remind you of things, people, or events you have loved in your life. Bring them to the circle. Tell the story of each thing as you place it on the altar.

◼ **Put your love in the ribbons.** Many pagans dance around the maypole as a way of weaving together all of the love and passion in their lives (traditionally, this celebration involved "fertility" rituals among adults). Take all of the ribbons for your maypole. Have everyone take turns putting their love into the ribbons. One by one you can pick them up and say, for example, "For the love of my cat," or "for the love of peace," or "for the love of my new friend," and so on. There are so many different kinds of love. See how many different things you can name to love. Pick ribbons that have colors that represent those things for you.

■ **Dance the maypole.** Any long pole can be stuck into the ground and used as a maypole—even a broom handle. If you don't have a place to put one into the ground, try attaching the knot at the top of the ribbons to the ceiling. You can also get short ribbons and braid them into personal bracelets and necklaces, still using the symbolism of the colors and of weaving together your visions. Have each person pick a color or colors that symbolize something that he or she wants to weave into his or her life. Have every other person take a step toward the center of the circle and stand facing the person on the outside circle. Each person on the inside of the circle will go under the ribbon of the person on the outside of the circle. They will then go over the next person's ribbon. Basically, those in the inside circle move clockwise, and those in the outside circle move counterclockwise, going over and under each other's ribbons until they are all wound to the bottom, where you can tie them together. Put on music. The song "Kore Chant" is by Lauren Liebling and Starhawk and is also sung on the CD *Chants: Ritual Music from Reclaiming and Friends.* (see page 80)

The Great Giveaway

Summer Solstice

Being Wiccan means that you can make magic. Today we're celebrating Summer Solstice. It's the end of June and the sun is bright and it's warm late into the evening. This morning, my friend Heather and I painted a big sign for our front lawn saying "The Great Witches' Summer Solstice Giveaway." There are lots of ways to celebrate Summer Solstice. Every single year, my family and I collect things we don't need anymore and give them away. Heather and I rub our hands together and cackle the way our friends at school think witches do. But we are cackling at the thought of the great magic our giveaway could make.

My mom says that we're giving things away because "we're finished with this stuff, so we give it to someone else, just like winter changes into summer." But I say giving things away is making magic.

Heather and I have been making friendship bracelets since Beltaine. Last night we had a sleepover and made so many that they're coming out of our ears. We set up a table with a special sign that says "Heather and Aisha's magic friendship bracelets." Soon people start coming by. "How much is this?" they ask, and "How much is that?" Every time we say, "It's free, it's free, everything's free," and their eyes bug out of their heads and they almost don't believe us. Making people's eyes bug out of their heads with happiness is a kind of magic.

Niko, a girl we know from school, walks up. Instead of asking how much things are, she bursts out, "What do you mean this is a witches' giveaway? Witches don't give things away. Witches ride broomsticks and wear pointy hats and cast magic spells and cackle and stuff like that!"

It's Summer Solstice—everything is big and bright and beautiful, but I don't know what to say. "Being a witch just means that we take care of the earth and each other," my mom begins, but Heather interrupts.

"Witches do make magic," Heather says, "but it's exactly the kind of magic that happens when you give things away. Want to stay and see?"

"Sure," Niko says, and she sits down at our table with us.

A man comes to look at our bracelets. He says, "These are beautiful. How much do you want for them?"

"They're free, they're free, everything's free!" Heather and I both yell. Niko laughs. At school she always laughs when Heather and I yell things at the same time. "But," Heather says, "they're friendship bracelets, so you'll have to give one to a friend."

"Perfect," the man says. "I want to give one to a friend who's moving so she'll remember her home here." He takes it and almost skips away.

Making an old man skip is a kind of magic.

"See?" Heather says to Niko.

"How much?" a little girl asks, and at the same time Heather and I say, "It's free, it's free, everything's free!" But this time Niko joins us. And we can't believe it, but the little girl gives the bracelet to her sister, who swings her, laughing wildly, up onto her shoulders. Sisters getting along that well is definitely a kind of magic. I know because not only am I Eli's sister, but Heather is over so much it's kind of like I'm her sister too.

All day long the sun pours down and people stream past our house and we say, "Free, they're free, everything's free." My parents give away old books, clothes, and lots of odds and ends. Heather and I give out bracelets: red bracelets, green bracelets, yellow bracelets, purple bracelets, rainbow bracelets—all different sizes and shapes. And Niko helps.

Then the most magical thing happens. We start to see people pass wearing our bracelets. People we didn't even give our bracelets to. Heather cackles her best cackle. I do too. "Since we're witches anyway," I tell Niko, "we might as well be able to cackle when we see magic!" And then Heather and Niko and I all cackle the best witchy cackles in the world. We cackle and chortle and chuckle until we fall out of our chairs and onto the grass. We lie there as the hot Summer Solstice sun gradually cools and the evening winds start to blow gently.

Niko sits up and asks, "Are all witches as silly and funny as you?"

"No," my dad answers.

"Not at all," my mom adds, "it's just the two of them." And we all have to admit they are absolutely, positively right.

Niko helps us pack up before she goes home. When the last of our things are gathered, we leave them outside in a box that says "Free," and then go set up our own little Summer Solstice ritual just for us.

We light candles in the backyard and make flower chains. With each flower we pick we make a promise about how we'll care for the earth or for each other. We make promises to recycle, to not drive the car everywhere, and things like that. Our flower chains grow long, and we drape them over our heads and around our wrists. Last of all, Heather and I make promises to be best-sister-friends forever, for the rest of our lives. After all, it's not every day you'd find such a wild, weird, and witchy friend to make magic with.

Things to Talk About

▪ Aisha and Heather call what happens when they give away bracelets "making magic." What kinds of magic do they make? Do you think those things are magic? What kinds of magical things have you done? What kinds of magical things could you do?

▪ Besides talking about making magic, Aisha and Heather cackle like witches. People at their school think witches do these things. Did you notice differences between what Aisha and Heather do as witches (people who are part of the Wiccan religion) and what children at your school think witches are and do?

- Have you ever had people misunderstand something about who you are and what you do? How have you dealt with it?

- Aisha says that Heather is her "best-sister-friend." She and Heather are family because they are close. Does your family include people you are not related to but love a lot? Does it include animals? Even trees or bodies of water?

Celebrations

- **Gather flowers.** Take your group out for a walk and gather all of the wildflowers you can find. If you do not have a place or time for this activity, you can ask everyone to bring half a dozen flowers, or a leader could pick up bunches. Tell some stories about where you found your plants and what they mean to you. See if you can find some information about the flowers you picked. It can be fun to look up books of native plants and see what traditionally grows on the land in your area. Many flowers can be eaten; see if you can find edible flowers and taste them. This can lead to conversations about sustainably growing and harvesting plants (see *One Makes the Difference: Inspiring Actions That Change Our World*, by Julia Butterfly Hill, on page 79). Put the flowers on your altar in several festively colored jars.

- **Find something to give away.** Before the ritual, put the names of everyone in your group into a hat. Group members will pull out a name and then find something they own that they are ready to part with and something they think the person whose name they picked might enjoy. Place each object on the altar. These things will be used in the ritual.

- **Give presents.** Go around the circle. Have each person give their gift and tell one thing about it that made it special to them and one way they hope it will be special for the person they are giving it to.

- **Create promise pictures.** All you will need is an iron, waxed paper, scissors, and the flowers. Ask each person to take one flower each and state what he or she will do to take care of the earth and others. Go around the circle as many times as needed until everyone has a bouquet. Then every person can cut out two identical sheets of waxed paper in any shape, arrange the flowers on one piece, put the second piece on top, and iron it until it sticks and is flat. You can hang your bouquets on walls, on altars, or in windows as reminders of your connection and partnership with the earth.

The Perfect Peace Harvest

Every year on Lammas, we clamor our way to City Hall with posters and placards to picket for peace. Every year since I was a baby we have a big rally. Speakers and singers, dancers and screamers, we all gather to say that we want "peace now, peace now." Lammas is a time to raise your voice, even when it's hard. It's a time to say "no" to war and to anything else that hurts anyone, anywhere in the world.

Most of the people at the rally aren't pagans, but they all yell "peace now, peace now," which is as much of a Lammas celebration as anything I can think of.

We carry drums to bang and cymbals to clang. Since I've been coming here all my life, it's not too hard to get ready to clang and bang. I come ready to make some noise.

On Lammas you've gotta stomp your dancing feet,

On Lammas you've gotta raise your voice and speak,
Lammas is the harvest, we've gotta harvest peace.

This year there are at least a hundred people, maybe more. There are people with canes, people with crowns, people draped in crazy costumes, yelling, "Peace now, peace now!"

There are people with puppets taller than the treetops and people holding signs that say "No War." Standing in back are people watching in silence until we all yell, "Peace now, peace now!" Then everyone yells together.

My family and I meet people under a banner that says, "Pagans for Peace." There are pagans we know who greet us with big happy hugs and pagans we don't know, but we all yell, "Peace now, peace now!" for Lammas.

On Lammas you've gotta stomp your dancing feet,
On Lammas you've gotta raise your voice and speak,
Lammas is the harvest, we've gotta harvest peace.

There are babies snug in their snuggly carriers and toddlers toddling on the grass. They yell, "eace, now, eace, now," which is definitely close enough to "peace now" for any of us. "That's how you used to say it when you were little," my dad tells me. My brother Eli yells and sings, and I swing him up onto my shoulders.

There is a stage at the front of the rally with microphones and banners. Huge flags with doves and peace signs wave in the August wind. There are old women in crazy hats who step up and sing for peace. But there are no kids up there. There are teenagers in silly skirts and socks who step up and cheer and chant for peace. But there are no kids. Everyone speaks out, but there are no kids at the microphones.

"This is ridiculous," I burst out to my mom. "I have been coming here my whole entire life and I've never seen a single kid on that stage!"

"Aisha," my mom says, "what a great idea! Run up and tell them you want to speak. Hurry!"

I freeze. I hadn't meant me. Just some kid. My heart thuds in my chest. I just meant someone, anyone, else. I look at the crowd: a hundred people, maybe more. I am ten years old. I do not want to speak in front of all of them.

But I have been coming here for ten years, and for ten years I've chanted the same words:

> On Lammas you've gotta stomp your dancing feet,
> On Lammas you've gotta raise your voice and speak,
> Lammas is the harvest, we've gotta harvest peace.

My stomach is fluttery. My legs are jittery. This feels nothing like peace, but I've got to do it. I know I do. So, I slowly lift my brother off of my shoulders and put him on the ground.

"I'm going to go up," I tell my mom, and she grins her biggest grin. "I'm going to go up!" I exclaim loudly to everyone around us under the "Pagans for Peace" banner. Our friend Alex comes over to me. "Hooray!" he yells. He picks me up in a big bear hug and swings me around. "Good for you!" our friends cheer. Now I have to do it.

I run all the way up to the stage before I can lose my nerve and run back. There are organizers standing next to it. "I am here to speak," I tell the grown-ups by the stage.

One man looks at me. "There isn't enough time," he says.

I want to run back but I don't. Instead, I take a deep breath and try again. "There are never any kids speaking," I tell him. Then I turn to the other organizers. "What if I only say just four quick things?" The organizers look at each other and shrug. "Okay," they say. "Just four quick things."

I stand at the microphone with my fluttery stomach and jittery legs. I have been coming here since I was a baby, but raising my voice in front of the whole crowd is one of the hardest things I've ever done. Even though I don't feel the littlest bit of peace, I take a deep breath and begin.

"War doesn't help anything," I say. "It doesn't give us clean water."

Everyone yells back, "No!"

"It doesn't give us land to grow our food!" I say.

And again, the crowd yells, "No!"

"It doesn't let kids grow up healthy!" I call out.

"No! No! No!" everyone yells.

"We all need the earth and the water, and we all need each other," I raise my voice loudly into the microphone. "So," I finish, "what do we want?"

And the crowd goes wild, yelling, "Peace now, peace now, peace now!"

I look down and see that our "Pagans for Peace" group is starting a big, snaking, twisting, spiral dance through the crowd. I run down and grab hands with them as more and more people join us, taking each other's hands and singing.

We sing and smile, dancing our way through the crowd and around the buildings. Our song fills me with bouncy gleefulness. With my legs strong and sturdy again, I imagine our song is like water splashing us.

On Lammas you've gotta stomp your dancing feet,
On Lammas you've gotta raise your voice and speak,
Lammas is the harvest, we've gotta harvest peace.

I have come here every Lammas since I was a baby, but speaking in front of the whole entire crowd is the most perfect peace harvest I've ever made.

Things to Talk About

Aisha and her family and friends have been going to the peace rally since she was a baby. Are there things that you do that you have done all your life because of your beliefs? What are they? Are there similarities between what you do and what Aisha's family does?

What are some of the reasons why Aisha thinks that war is wrong? Are there other effects of war? Are there other things that create these problems? What skills do you have that you could use to help work toward better solutions?

▪ Aisha notices that it is unfair that no children ever speak out at the rally. She speaks up even though it's scary. What helped her do this (for example, taking deep breaths and getting grounded, telling other people who would encourage her, and acting fast before she lost her nerve)?

▪ Have you ever done something that was scary for you? What things did you do for yourself to help you face your fear?

Celebrations

▪ **Find heroes.** Find pictures of people who have stood up for what they believed in and made a difference in the world. See if you can find contemporary people, particularly pagans, who, through their spiritual beliefs, practices, and actions, give us examples of how this faith and its rituals can empower people to make positive change. People who aren't well known can be heroes as well. Do you have a brave family member? A fabulously outspoken person in your community? Ask people in your group to bring pictures of their own heroes and discuss why these people are inspiring as they put the photos on the altar.

▪ **Be a hero.** Find out about an antiwar campaign that calls or writes letters to local politicians. As a group, write letters urging your representatives to take a stand for peace. Place these letters on your altar for the ritual.

▪ **Meditate.** Sit or lie down comfortably and close your eyes. Take a deep breath and imagine a fire starting down at the base of your spine. It feels warm and soothing through your belly. It is like sitting, relaxed, in front of a bonfire, but the fire is you, it is your spirit. Keep breathing deeply as the fire begins to spread across your back and up through your chest, filling you with energy. Take another deep breath as the fire continues to move up through your neck and out through your head. Imagine this fire clearing your thoughts and allowing you to feel comfortable and sure of yourself and what you believe. You are able to listen and learn from others and share what you know with strength. As you continue to breathe, imagine this fire spreading down your arms and out your fingertips. Imagine doing the work you love most with your favorite people. Imagine all that you create and all that you touch becoming moved by your fiery spirit. Let yourself sigh. Imagine your fire moving down past your hips and through your feet. This is your spirit and the wise spirit of the Goddess. You are part of what is sacred in the world. This fire guides your feet and helps you know what path you are meant to walk. Still taking deep breaths, see yourself as glowing with this fire within. How will this fire move into the world? Where will it take you? Imagine yourself doing what matters most to you, something you feel will make a difference in the world. Let the picture form clearly in your mind. Watch what it looks like, who you are with, what you are doing, what you smell, what you hear, what you feel. This is you. You have this power within you. Breathe deeply. Allow the fire to move back up your legs, back through your arms, down from your head and chest, until it glows at the base of your spine again. Sigh out all the extra energy you don't need and imagine it sinking back into the earth, which knows what to do with it. Breathe deeply, return to this room, and open your eyes.

Paint your vision. Get a large roll of paper. Each person can take a turn lying on the paper. Trace each person, and cut out each tracing. Make sure there are enough paints and paintbrushes for everyone. Then paint the pictures you saw during the meditation. For example, you may want to paint all flames, or you may want to paint some flames along with some pictures of the things you do.

Aisha's Magic Moonlit Walk

It's so early it's still dark.

I tiptoe out of bed to go for my magic moonlit walk.

I have a big sack I've filled with magic things for Fall Equinox.

You have to have a big sack when you go on a magic moonlit walk.

Each one of my magic things comes from one of the holidays I celebrated over the past year.

My parents are away for Fall Equinox. I am staying at Alex's big house by the ocean.

It's so early it's still dark.

Even though Alex knows I'll be going for this walk, I still close the door extra quietly when I go outside to the yard.

I have a big long black cape.

You have to have a big long cape to go for a magic moonlit walk.

The nice thing about having a friend

who has a house by the ocean is that you can go for magic moonlit walks in the back-yard and be safe, even when it's so early in the morning.

It is so early it's still dark.

I stand outside on the deck behind the house and breathe the ocean air.

It's Fall Equinox. Our next holiday will be Samhain.

Today we celebrate the final fall harvest, and I want to celebrate it alone—if you can even call it alone when the ocean roars.

I reach up my hands and close my eyes. I remember the salty tears I cried for so long after Milly died, and how I still miss her even though I don't cry for her anymore. I take out Milly's old ball and hold it for a moment. Every time I hold it, I feel the love I shared with Milly. "Thank you, Ocean Goddess," I whisper, and goose bumps run up and down my arms.

You have to whisper to the Ocean Goddess and get goose bumps on a magic moon-lit walk.

It's so early it's still dark. I walk over to a patch of big pine and cedar trees. I press against a cedar trunk and let the gnarled bark make imprints on the side of my face. I remember the wind and how it blew through the pine trees last Winter Solstice, when Heather and I were fighting. "Thank you, tree spirits, for helping me make up with peo-ple," I say out loud. It wouldn't be a magic moonlit walk if you didn't thank the tree spir-its at least once.

Then I lean into the big cedar and slide down till I'm sitting right on the ground. It's a chilly morning so I pull my cape tight. On both my arms I'm wearing the friendship bracelets that Heather and I made. "Thank you, Mother Earth, for so many good friends," I whisper to the ground.

Maybe I'm not really all by myself.

If I were a wood sprite I would sleep on the pine needles every night, just me and the earth. I pull the hood of my cape over my head and lie down on the ground.

At some point on a magic moonlit walk, you have to be a wood sprite.

Lying under the dark sky, I listen and watch as the day gets ready to come. If I were a wood sprite, seagulls and ocean waves and wind through the trees would be my lullabies. But the wind starts to blow cold. Chilly whooping ocean wind nips and bites my ears. Maybe I won't be a wood sprite after all. Maybe I'll get up and see where the wind takes me and what treasure I'll remember as I walk there.

You have to listen for the best place to move next on a magic moonlit walk.

Standing with my ears cold in the wind I remember that I've brought along the great big hat I wore in our Spring Equinox play. I take it out of my bag and put it on my head. I start to walk under the gray-blue sky in my cape and big crazy hat. "Thank you, spirits of the wind, for helping me put on plays," I say. But that isn't all I want to say. I keep walking through the wind. It blows harder. "And for helping me speak my mind when I need to most!" I yell, leaning into the wind, letting it hold me up. The wind bounces the sound of my voice back at me.

It is always good to yell something at the top of your lungs on a magic moonlit walk, if there is any way you possibly can.

I remember riding through the wind to watch Rupie's cat have kittens. Now my own kitten is almost full grown. I turn and face the ocean and take my kitten's catnip mouse out of my bag. "Thank you, Ocean Goddess, for my new cat, Kali." That is the last thing in my bag. I hold it and sigh a big sigh. I run back through the wind to the house. When I get to the porch I see the sun beginning to bring its fire to the sky. There is a red line coming up from the ocean.

Seeing the sun rise is the perfect way to end a magic moonlit walk.

Last time I was at Alex's house, it was Beltaine and the sun was bright and hot. I hold my arms up to the sunrise again and remember how we ran around in the ocean with the sun beating down on our backs. "Thank you," I call out to the sun. It feels so right that I'm standing on the porch with the sun and the wind and the waves and the trees and the dirt. I put my arms around myself again. "And thanks to me," I whisper to myself last of all. Because it wouldn't be a real magic moonlit walk if you didn't thank yourself too.

Things to Talk About

■ What makes this ritual different from the rituals in the other stories? How have you celebrated holidays? Do you like celebrating in different ways for different occasions or moods?

- Aisha celebrates this ritual alone. But at one point in the story, she states that she is not really alone. What does she mean? Have you ever felt that way?

- At another point in the story, Aisha imagines that she is a wood sprite. What kind of things have you pretended? Have these things ever felt magical or sacred to you?

- Aisha walks without knowing where she will go next. Instead, she just listens. Why would she do this? Have you ever done anything like that?

Celebrations

- **Make magic moonlight sacks.** Find or make enough cloth sacks for every person in your group to have one. Two squares of cloth sewn together on three sides with a ribbon to hold the top shut make a good sack, as fancy as it needs to be. These bags will be used to go for your own magic moonlit walk. Get a piece of white cloth for each person. Have enough fabric felts or paints for everyone. The cloths will become your "wheel of the year" crests. Design each one as your symbol of the wheel of the year. For example, some people might draw the four seasons in a circle, and others may wish to draw phases of the Goddess/God or of the moon. Sew or pin the crests onto your sacks and place them on your altar.

- **Fill your magic moonlight sacks.** In the story, Aisha pulls something out of her sack that reminds her of each holiday that she has celebrated all year.

Find a symbol for each holiday you have celebrated. If you haven't been celebrating the holidays throughout the year, gather things that symbolize your journey through the seasons. These things can all be placed in your sacks or on and around your altar.

Make capes. Gather enough brightly colored clothes so that every person can choose a favorite color. Pull the "cape" around your shoulders and fasten it. Put the things you collected in your bag and carry it with you for your magic moonlit walk.

Go for a magic moonlit walk. If you can, go out around sunrise or sunset. If your group has a set meeting time, see if you can find a special and beautiful place outdoors. The walk can also be done in your local park or even in your building. You may wish to decorate your space in a way that is special and out of the ordinary. If you are in a room, for example, decorate the corners in a way that reflects different seasons. As a group, go on a magic moonlit walk similar to Aisha's. Give everyone an opportunity to decide which direction to walk. Find ways to inspire the group to think of different places to go. This can be done by making comments such as "can you feel the breeze?" or "should we follow it?" At each stopping place, take objects that have significance for you out of your bag. Different people will be reminded of different directions at every point. This is fine. These walks will have a natural beginning and end.

Guide for Parents and Educators

Ritual elements that are common to all pagan celebrations include decorating an altar, grounding, cleansing, casting a circle, and opening a circle. Within this structure, you can customize your practice as needed for your group and the celebration. This section is an overview of the basics of pagan worship, which you can use to create a sacred space for sharing the stories in this book and for honoring the seasonal holidays together, even if you have no experience with these traditions. These suggestions are intentionally simple so that children can learn to do them on their own.

Decorating an Altar

Every chapter in this book includes ideas for altar-decorating activities that are specific to each holiday, but altars usually have more on them than decorations for one particular event. Many of the objects on a pagan's altar are designed to help with the aspects of casting a circle. Some of the most common altar items are:

- Candles for the four directions—When you cast your circle, you will call on the spirits of the North, South, East, and West. You may light a candle for each direction as it is invoked. The colors of the candles correspond with the four directions. For example, green is for the North and earth, white is for the East and air, red is for the South and fire, and blue is for the West and water. You may wish to pick other colors that best symbolize the elements for you. You can also place objects that symbolize each direction next to each candle. You may put bark and plants facing North, feathers and incense facing East, love letters and symbols of your creative work facing South, and shells and smooth stones facing West.

- A five-pointed star (pentacle)—Many pagans put an image of the pentacle on their altars facing North. The five points symbolize the four directions/elements, with the fifth, the spirit, being brought into balance when we are in right relationship with the other four. It also symbolizes the life cycle: birth, adolescence, adulthood, aging, and death, coming back around to rebirth or regeneration.

- A sacred bowl—This bowl holds the water for your saltwater purification. It is placed on the west side of your altar, and it symbolizes the sacred womb of the Goddess.

- A double-edged ritual knife (athame)—The athame is associated with air and is placed on the east side of your altar. It can be used to stir saltwater and to draw invoking/devoking pentacles that "cut" the sacred space of a circle. You can also use a wand or your finger.

- A wand—Wands are linked with fire and with conducting the flow of energy. Any pleasing stick you find and dedicate to this purpose works well.

- Symbols of the Goddess or God—A chalice or special candle is often placed at the center of an altar for the Goddess or God. Any objects you find that symbolize aspects of the Goddess/God for you are fine.

The most important thing to know about the altar is that it is your space to put symbols of what matters most to you. Anything that holds a place of honor in your life is appropriate.

Grounding

You will want to begin any ritual by doing a grounding meditation. When we cast a circle, we want to be grounded, to feel strong in our connection to our bodies and to the earth's body. In pagan traditions, the body is not seen as a hindrance to our relationship to the divine; all life is sacred, including ourselves. If we are not grounded, ritual can leave us feeling scattered and unfocused. Grounding helps us to bring our whole selves into ritual and to keep the ritual rooted in the world, not separate from action. The ability to become grounded is a very powerful skill to teach children. It can help them develop body awareness and help them to deal with intense emotions and difficult situations. There are many ways to get grounded. The following meditation is useful for beginners:

Stand or sit in a way that is comfortable for you. Breathe deeply. Imagine branches coming out of your feet, the bones you sit on, your fingers, and the top of your head and going deep down into the center of the earth. Every time you breathe out, you send whatever you don't need, any feeling you do not want, down into the earth, which knows what to do with it. Every time you breathe in, draw up what you need from the earth. Do you need to feel comforted? Do you need wisdom? The earth will give that to you. Each breath draws this energy through every part of you. Feel it spread through your feet, your knees, your legs. Feel it in your hips. Feel it in your belly. Silently name the parts of your body where you can feel this loving, healing energy. When you feel all your worries drain out and the earth energy in every inch of yourself, imagine your roots and branches slowly moving up and back into you. Put your hands on the ground and feel any extra energy you don't need drain into it. Stand up and shake your sillies out. Feel your strong connection to the earth!

Cleansing

Once we are grounded, we want to clear ourselves of our habitual way of being in the world so that we can make a space for "magic," for being able to shift our consciousness. When we cast a circle we make a space where we can feel safe, protected, and healed by the earth. It is also a space for transformation, where we can know the extent of our personal power and be empowered to use our gifts to bring healing back to the earth and to each other. A circle is a space of mystery where we can feel closest to the Goddess/God. We cleanse ourselves in order to let go of the things that distract us from this connection—like a fight with a friend, worries about a test, stress about our health, or any other concerns that are on our minds. Cleansing is a powerful tool for children, since it helps them learn to let go of what is not useful to them at that moment and develop an ability to be present. The following activity, called salt purification, is one of many ways to cleanse, and it can be a particularly fun one for young people:

> In a special bowl, mix sea salt counterclockwise with your finger, a wand, or an athame (see page 62). As Hilary Valentine writes in *The Twelve Wild Swans*, this makes "our own little ocean to bathe in." Dip your fingers into your "little ocean" and sprinkle it over your bodies. Chant what you want to let go of—for example, "unfair brother"—or state what you want to feel—"giddy, happy, spring is here!" People can either sprinkle water over themselves or over the person standing next to them. This can be a fun, playful activity, especially outside in the summer sun. Picture swimming in the ocean; imagine each drop that touches you being the spray of an ocean wave and part of the Goddess/God. Imagine each drop as the Goddess/God helping to clear your mind and body to be ready for magic. You are now in this moment, not lingering in the past or jumping into the future. Feel what it is like to be present and clear, knowing you are a sacred being.

Casting a Circle

After grounding and cleansing, you are ready to cast a circle. When we do a ritual, we are raising power and energy. Casting a circle draws a safe space to do this. It allows us to raise the kind of energy we need and to be intentional about what we are drawing into our lives and our world. When we cast a circle, we draw a sacred space around us by invoking the spirits of the four directions: North, which is linked to earth and our bodies; East, which is linked to air and our minds; South, which is linked to fire and our sensuous/creative spirits; and West, which is linked to water and our emotions. The following circle invocation uses meditation, physical movement, and verbal invitation:

Stand facing North. Imagine you are lying on the floor of a forest cathedral. Let your back sink into the dirt, feel the leaves and needles of the forest floor, smell the deep soil. Imagine dancing on a hill in the moonlight. Imagine the feeling of the earth beneath your feet as you dance. Begin to move your body however you want, as if you are dancing with the spirits of the earth and celebrating together. Say, "Welcome, spirits of the ancient mountains, and giant wise trees. Welcome, spirits of the rich soil that grows our food!"

Walk around the circle until you are facing East. Pretend you are standing on a ferry and feeling the wind whip through your hair. It blows gently at times and then so powerfully that you lean into it and it holds you up.

What smells come to you in the wind? Let the wind invite you to play. Begin to move like the wind. How do your wind-arms move? How does your wind-back move? Your wind-chest? Your wind-legs? Say, "Welcome, gentle breezes that clear our minds. Welcome, powerful storms that shake us up when we're stuck. Welcome, spirits of movement and change!"

Walk around the circle until you are facing South. Imagine standing by a big bonfire. Each spark gives us a new idea; each flame fills us with deep love and excitement. Hear the fire crackle. Smell the smoke and draw its heat right into your body. Listen as the fire invites you to become your own fire. Begin to let your body spark and fly and move like the fire. Say, "Welcome, creative flickering flames. Welcome, flying sparks, burn bright in us."

Walk around the circle until you are facing West. Now you are jumping into a running river. It is cold and refreshing. It babbles and ripples and you let it carry you. Feel your emotions running like a river. Love the river and the part of yourself that can feel like a flowing river. You ride the river until it merges with a lake. You swim to the middle of the lake and sit on a rock and stare into its clear, still water. Imagine your emotions sitting motionless like the lake. Love the lake and the part of you that is still like the lake. Feel the water inviting you to move with it. Become your own body of water. How does water move through you? Are you crashing ocean waves or a long winding stream? Say, "Welcome, great Goddess of the waters, welcome, source of all life!"

Continue to walk around the circle until you reach North again, then walk to the center. Invite the Goddess/God to the center of your circle. Calling in the Goddess and God is simple. For example, if you wish to invite the crone aspect of the Goddess, you can picture a wise old woman and say, "Welcome Grandmother, bringer of wisdom!" The Goddess is often thought to embody three phases: maiden, mother, and crone. These phases manifest themselves in different phases of the moon as well as in the seasons of the year and in the different stages of our lives. The God is also often thought to embody phases, dying in the winter to be reborn as the sun. All life has a spirit that is part of the same source. We talk about different spirits and the Goddess and God, but we know that this source goes beyond any form. We use different names not because we see the divine as fragmented but in order to manifest an aspect of what we need to be close to in our lives and to recognize that there are many different ways to see divinity.

Remaining at the center of your circle, state, "As above, so below," imagining your safe, sacred space extending around you on all sides.

Some pagans draw five-pointed stars, or pentacles, in the air when casting a circle. You draw a pentacle by starting from the top peak and moving first to the bottom left, in the same way children usually draw stars. Drawing pentacles in the air in this way invokes the spirits you are calling in each direction.

Know that you are now protected and safe on all sides of yourself. You are in the middle of the sacred sources of the universe.

Opening the Circle

When we cast a circle, we close sacred space around us. When we finish a ritual, it is important to open that space back up. We want to release the spirits that we have called. Devocation, or letting go of what we've invoked, leaves us ready to take our energy back into our daily lives in the physical world. Devocation is simple; just work your way backward around the circle, thanking and saying farewell to the spirits who have been with you.

Stand facing West. Imagine swimming out of the water and back onto dry land. Say, "Thank you, West, for your protection and guidance. Hail and farewell!" Wave and blow kisses. Know that this energy is always inside you in some way, whether you are in a circle or not.

Walk until you are facing South. Feel the fire becoming a warm glow in your abdomen. See the bonfire mellow into coals. Repeat the same farewell.

Walk until you are facing East. Imagine the ferry, where the wind was blowing, moving to the shore. You climb off and all is still. Repeat the same farewell.

Walk until you are facing North. Stand for one moment on your hill. Feel the calm presence of the earth. Repeat the same farewell.

Have everyone in your group join hands and stand in a circle. Imagine your circle opening up over your head and under your feet. Call your thanks and wave and blow kisses to whatever Goddesses/Gods you have invited. Take a step in and swing your arms over your head. Call out, "The circle is open, but unbroken. Merry meet, merry part, and merry meet again!"

Touch the earth again and let your extra energy drain into the ground so it won't stay inside and make you feel agitated. Get some clear water and wash your hands.

If you drew a pentacle in the air when casting the circle, draw it in reverse, starting at the bottom left point and moving first to the top peak.

Make sure to always have fun food and drinks after your ritual. Magic can make people hungry, and food helps get you grounded in the physical world again.

Pagan Ethics

The stories and activities in this book touch on a few core pagan values, which help keep our spiritual practices ethical and make sure we work for good in the world. At the end of spells, most pagans say, "By the power of three-by-three, and harm it none, so mote it be." These words signify the three basic tenets of pagan ethics:

- The most fundamental ethic in the pagan tradition is to "harm none." No matter what we do, we strive not to harm any other living being. Our sense of right and wrong does not come from a book or an authority outside ourselves. Instead it comes from learning to listen to our own intuition while making sure that all we work toward is well intentioned and kind.

- Pagans believe that whatever we do, we draw back into our lives threefold. For some this is a karmic warning that what we do will be returned to us. For others, it is a belief that what we do to others affects us more than it does anyone else. Either way, this means that if we give healing, we heal ourselves, and if we contribute to destruction, we destroy ourselves. This principle helps guide us to ask only for what is good for everyone and everything around us. It helps us to recognize that reaching for the greatest good is our best reward.

- Pagan ritual focuses on raising power. This is a personal power that helps, as opposed to hinders, others in finding their own power. We do not work to change other people but rather to shift energy in our own lives and find what we need for ourselves.

These are traditions that welcome playful silliness and fun. The suggestions in this chapter are not meant to stifle your practice. Rather, they are tools to help you open the doorway of this spiritual path and discover a greater sense of personal freedom and authenticity.

Pagan Holidays

Samhain (October 31)

On Samhain we celebrate our continuing connection to and affection for our beloved dead. It is the pagan New Year, when the veil between the world of the living and the world of the dead is believed to be thinnest. It honors the Crone Goddess, who gives us wisdom, and the Horned God, who teaches us that death leads to new life. We see this expressed in "Thank You, Milly!" when Aisha's connection to her dog remains and helps her heal after the dog has died.

These pagan concepts are touched on in this story:

- The role of the four directions, earth, air, fire, and water, and their corresponding relationships to our bodies, minds, spirits, and emotions
- The act of casting a circle and making sacred space
- Honoring our emotions and moods, and understanding that they shift

Winter Solstice (December 20–23)

Winter Solstice is the darkest night of the year. This holiday teaches us to embrace the night. At the same time, this is a holiday of hope, because after Winter Solstice the nights get shorter, and the sun starts to return. It is a time to look within ourselves for insight. We see this expressed in "The Longest Night" when Aisha, after a terrible fight with her best friend, Heather, turns inward to find the source of the problem and its solution.

These pagan concepts are touched on in this story:

- Valuing dreams and intuition
- Not working to have power over others but instead changing ourselves
- The richness of chosen family and community

Brigid's Day (February 2)

Brigid's Day honors the sun's return with a festival of lights. The goddess Brigid is the midwife and teacher of creativity. This holiday celebrates initiation, being ready to understand and become part of life's mysteries in a new way. We see this expressed in "New Kittens" as Aisha's determination to overcome her fear of blood in order to witness the birth of kittens.

These pagan concepts are touched on in this story:

- Creativity as a powerful and life-giving force
- Asking for help and inspiration when stuck with a problem

Spring Equinox (March 20–23)

Spring Equinox celebrates the balance of day and night. It is a time of balance in our lives, reminding us to welcome new things and to say good-bye to things we want to leave behind. The Spring Equinox honors the maiden goddess Eostar (Easter, in Christian tradition), who is connected to fertility and rebirth. It honors the Spring God, who is also known as the fool, or trickster, reminding us to embrace life with joyful, playful exuberance. We see this theme expressed in "Our Rainy Day Play" through the balance of challenge and opportunity that Aisha and Heather face when it rains on the day of their play. We see it also in their resolve to embrace the rain and do the play anyway.

These pagan concepts are touched on in this story:

- Grounding yourself through breathing and connecting to the earth
- Honoring events in your life by collecting symbols of them for your sacred altar

Beltaine (May 1)

Beltaine, a time of fertility and growth, celebrates how our sexuality, spirituality, and creativity are all part of the same sacred source. During Beltaine, we celebrate this source within us as well as within all plants, animals, and life. It honors the Goddess and the God as the lovers of all things. They remind us to respect and protect our bodies and the earth's body. We see this expressed in "The Sea Creatures" through the ways that various characters love themselves and others. For the children, Beltaine is the celebration of friendship, of joy in their bodies, and of their connection to nature. For the adults, romantic and sexual love is part of what makes Beltaine a holy day.

These pagan concepts are touched on in this story:

- The maypole as part of a ritual bringing people together in spiritual community
- The use of water as a cleansing and grounding tool after ritual
- The sharing of food as part of ritual and celebration
- Colors as sacred symbols
- Ecstatic, joyful dance as part of ritual

Summer Solstice (June 20–23)

Summer Solstice celebrates the generosity of the universe during this bright time of year. Over the next season, the days will start getting shorter in preparation for the harvest. On Summer Solstice we can give away what is no longer useful to us to make room for the new in our lives. This holiday recognizes the transformative power of generosity and celebrates this transformation as something magical. This theme is expressed in "The Great Giveaway" when the magic of Summer Solstice transforms all who experience it.

These pagan concepts are touched on in this story:
- Caring for the earth and each other
- The idea of chosen families

Lammas (August 1)

Lammas is celebrated when some of the things in our gardens and in our lives begin to be ready for harvest, and some still need to be tended carefully. Lammas celebrates our connection to the Goddess and God through our responsibility to work for the kinds of things we would like to see harvested in the world. Lammas honors the Mother Goddess, who helps us do what we need to do even when it it difficult or scary. Lammas also honors the Sun God, Lough, who helps us use our skills and visions to work for the freedom of everyone. We see this reflected in "The Perfect Peace Harvest," when Aisha learns to speak up for what she believes in, even though she is nervous.

These pagan concepts are touched on in this story:
- The ethic of doing no harm
- Our responsibility to be active in shaping the kind of world we want

Fall Equinox (September 20–23)

Fall Equinox honors the balance of day and night as we continue through the wheel of the year. It celebrates moving into the mysteries of the dark. This holiday honors the Goddess as the "old one," a wise woman who helps us rest from the hard work of the whole year. It honors the God as the son of the Mother Goddess, who has found freedom. We see this expressed in "Aisha's Magic Moonlit Walk" in Aisha's creation of her own ritual to celebrate her accomplishments of the past year.

These pagan concepts are touched on in this story:

- Seeing spirit in everything, including yourself
- Coming full circle in our lives and honoring that journey

To Find Out More

Books

Amber, K. *Pagan Kids' Activity Book*. Horned Owl Publishing, 1998.

Baker, Dianne, Anne Hill, and Starhawk. *Circle Round: Raising Children in Goddess Traditions*. Bantam Books, 2000.

Johnson, Cait, and Maura D. Shaw. *Celebrating the Great Mother: A Handbook of Earth-Honoring Activities for Parents and Children*. Destiny Books, 1995.

Hill, Julia Butterfly. *One Makes the Difference: Inspiring Actions That Change Our World*. HarperSanFrancisco, 2002.

O'Gaea, Ashleen. *Pagan Parenting: Teaching the Wiccan Faith to Children*. New Page Books, 2002.

Madden, Kristin. *Pagan Parenting: Spiritual, Magical and Emotional Development of the Child*. Llewellyn Publications, 2000.

McVickar Edwards, Carolyn. *The Storyteller's Goddess: Tales of the Goddess and Her Wisdom from Around the World*. HarperCollins, 1991.

Starhawk. *The Spiral Dance: A Rebirth of the Ancient Religion of the Great Goddess*. HarperSanFrancisco, 1999.

Starhawk, and Hilary Valentine. *Twelve Wild Swans: A Journey into the Realm of Magic, Healing and Action*. HarperSanFrancisco, 2000.

Music

Hill, Anne. *Circle Round and Sing: Songs for Family Celebrations in Goddess Traditions.* Serpentine Music, 2000.

Libana. *A Circle Is Cast.* Spinning, 1986.

Reclaiming Collective. *Chants: Ritual Music from Reclaiming and Friends.* Reclaiming Records, 1997.

Reclaiming Collective. *Let It Begin Now: Music from the Spiritual Dance.* Reclaiming Collective Music, 2001.

Websites/Groups

Circle of Life Foundation: www.circleoflife.org

Covenant of Unitarian Universalist Pagans (CUUPS): www.cuups.org

Reclaiming Collective: www.reclaiming.org

Acknowledgments

This book would not be possible without the love, support, and ingenious feedback of my beloved friends and chosen family: Joyelle Brandt, Miriam Cooper, Angie Doekson, Katy Einbleau, Krista Drommer, Gita Joshi, Mikaela Huesser, and Amy Salmon. My deepest gratitude and love to all of you.

Huge thanks also go out to the wonderful REACH listserve of Unitarian Universalist religious educators across the continent. Dozens of people from this community have given their enthusiasm and encouragement since the very beginning stages of this work. I would particularly like to thank those who spent time reviewing drafts of each story: Connie Dunn, Eric Hinkle, Paula Gonzales, Ellyn Lentz, Kelly Masters-Quinn, Joan McDonald, Carol Rudisill, and Cyndi Whitmore.

Last, I would like to thank Mary Benard, Betsy Martin, Suzanne Morgan, and Ari McCarthy of Skinner House Books for all of their support and skills throughout the publishing process.